MW01047366

Redeemed

Michelle Rabon

Printed in the U.S.A.

ISBN-13: 978-0692172841
ISBN-10: 069217284X

Dear Friend,

The glitter of the lights dance around the tree. The air is filled with the essence of cinnamon and apples, and the crisp bite of cold air pierces my nose and sinks deep into my chest. My heart cannot contain the joy that wells up within me at this time of the year, *this girl loves Christmas*.

My most cherished memories have been formed in this season, memories sometimes marked by uncertainty and sadness. Whether final Christmas' with loved ones or first Christmas' with new additions, these memories shape what I love about Christmas. Looking back over my life I cannot remember a Christmas season that wasn't filled with joy. Yet somehow no matter what we faced that year, happiness always finds a way to sneak in.

The joyous feeling of the Christmas season isn't dependent on my emotions. It is, however, completely centered-around the birth of Christ. Jesus Christ came to live as flesh and dwell with us and ultimately redeem mankind. This is where the truth of Christmas rises to the surface. We experience the glory of the season because we know it ultimately has nothing to do with us.

Advent marks the twenty-five liturgical days leading up to Christmas. (The word *liturgical* comes from the word *liturgy* which refers to the act of Christian worship.) Advent is twenty-five days of worship preceding Christmas Day. It is a time to focus our hearts and minds, to shut out the noise of the world and rush of the season, and rest in a deeper connection with Christ.

This Advent study will not focus on the traditional Christmas story, but instead will walk with the women of Scripture who were directly affected by His life. Their transforming testimonies of redemption brings to life the impact of why Christ came for us. He didn't come to stay a baby in a manger, He came to be our Savior. His purpose was far beyond the cries in the stillness of that night in the stable. He came to redeem what was lost.

Each day we will read about a new woman from Scripture and explore the effect of Christ on her life. Scripture reading, study points, guided questions and devotions will take your study of each woman deeper. As we watch God change her life, we will see that He too, can change ours.

Write out your prayer for this Advent season: Ask for BIG and BOLD faith, seek our precious SAVIOR in the pages of Scripture, and knock on the door of hope this Advent.

_____

_____

_____

_____

_____

_____

_____

_____

_____

_____

What's inside...

"As for our redeemer, the Lord of hosts is his name, the Holy One of Israel."

Isaiah 47:4 KJV

Scripture Reading:
Genesis 3

Deeper Study:
Genesis 2
2 Corinthians 11:3
1 Timothy 2:13

I get it. You are thinking, "Please tell me what on earth Eve has to do with Christmas?" I don't want us to rush past another Christmas and not witness the testimony of what Christ came to do. Eve may not have been alive during the time Christ walked the Earth, but she began the downward spiral that became the reason why He needed to come in the first place.

The opening act is set in the Garden; Adam and Eve living in perfect paradise fell prey to the enemy. He cunningly deceived Eve, but Adam willfully chose to disobey God's command (Genesis 2:17). Those are the cliff notes, but the ramifications of their choices extend to the entire world and every single person to be born for the rest of time.

Fortunately, Eve's story didn't end with the tragedy of the fall of man or the eviction from the Garden. It also didn't end with the death of her righteous son, Abel. Her story was the beginning, a prelude to God's plan of redemption.

Jesus.

He was and is the answer for all sin, for all time.

God sent Him with a purpose He knew from the beginning. The transgressions in the garden tipped the first domino over. Each piece collapsing on the other throughout history leading up to the cross of Christ.

Without the fall of man there would have been no need for His sacrifice on a splintered cross. There would have been no need for Mary to deliver her Son in a stable, or wise men to seek the King. There would have been no agony, desperation or sin in this life.

Eve teaches us many things, but redemption is by far one of the greatest.

Despite her sin, God's amazing grace was set into motion. He fully clothed her and Adam's naked bodies and looked to His Son who would ultimately be the one to fully cover all shame.

When Eve walked out of the Garden, body and mind broken by sin, she couldn't forsee the plan to come. She didn't know that she would bare a son out of her heartbreak that would begin a righteous line which would bring forth the Savior.

Despite her sin, God allowed her to still be a part of His story.

This woman perfectly crafted by God's hands needed Christ's beautiful act of redemption and so do we.

How has Christ "fully covered" your shame?

Notes:

He will remember your sins no more - justify grace

How do we forgive ourselves

where did the serpent come from?

God gives us "free will"

Scripture Reading:
Joshua 2:1-3
Joshua 6:17-25

Deeper Study:
Matthew 1:5-6
Hebrews 11:30-31

Four women from the Old Testament play a significant role in the lineage of Christ. Each one lacking the perfection one would think was necessary to be a part of Jesus's story. After all, He is the King of Kings. But, here is what I love about God; He was not repelled by their past or ours because He has the power to change your future.

Eve was deceived.

Ruth was lost.

Bathsheba was unfaithful.

And Rahab was a prostitute. _first woman of Jesus lineage_

Yet, despite their choices, they teach us redemption isn't conditional on your former transgressions. It is, however, determined by where you put your hope for the future.

Rahab couldn't have foreseen the plan of God, but choosing to say yes to two Israelite spies would greatly alter her future. God was not unknown to the people of Jericho, in fact, most cultures knew of Israel's God and all He had done. Just because they chose to worship other gods didn't mean they had never heard of the one true God.

Rahab heard of how He parted the Red Sea to rescue His children. She likely also knew of the wilderness wonderings and the battles fought and won by the hand of God.

Rahab was defined by a shamed profession and was clearly looking for hope outside the Jericho walls. Hope that could only be found in God. She believed that if God wanted Jericho, He would have it. Her faith was what rescued her and her family from destruction when the walls of Jericho fell.

What has negatively defined you in your past that made you long for a future hope?

Certainly it was more than literal walls that God destroyed around Rahab. In His sovereignty He placed her within the lineup that led to the birth of Christ. She married Salomon and gave birth to a son. Her son, Boaz, would redeem a young woman named Ruth. Who, in turn, would have a son named Obed, who would have a son named Jesse, the father of David. The beautiful lineage that led to Christ was no mistake, it was crafted with purpose. Each of these Old Testament women teach us that the pages of Scripture illustrate the Christmas story in the most beautiful way. They illustrate what it took to get to the manger and eventually to get to the cross and the empty grave.

What walls has He removed in your life?

Notes:

_____

_____

_____

Ruth

Scripture Reading:
Ruth 4

Deeper Study:
Ruth 1-3
Matthew 1:5

From a culture known for leading Israelite men away from God comes a woman who teaches us much about devotion. The Moabites knew of the God of the Jews and had heard the stories of His protection and care, yet didn't believe in Him. Ruth's culture and traditions lead us to assume certain things about her, but the fact is *God changed her future*. Just because our story doesn't start well, doesn't mean God won't finish it with redemption.

There is no doubt that God allowed the elements of Ruth's story to unfold with the purpose of using her life. A mother in law of the faith and a city of great significance became the landing place for Ruth after loosing it all. I think the beauty we find in this is that Ruth seemed to know there was no hope in staying behind, the only hope she had was moving forward and choosing God.

On a dusty road, when told to return to her people and her ~~gods~~ Gods, Ruth chose Naomi. She chose the only true God. She may not have known what her future would hold, but she knew there was a greater hope ahead.

Looking forward what is your great hope?

We know the story doesn't end with her stepping across the threshold of Bethlehem. Surprisingly, an unforgettable love story unfolds. A story of pure grace in human form is woven into Ruth's life, and for you and I a picture is painted of Christ's love for us. God in His great sovereignty allowed this Moabite woman to be a part of His redemptive plan. He used Boaz and Ruth to further the line of David which would prophetically lead to the birth of Jesus.

The need for Christ began long before He was laid in a manger. Long before His first earthly cries, God was preparing the way for His people to receive His Son. God was paving a way to bring Him into the world at the right time, for all mankind. As for Ruth, choosing God on that dusty road meant that her life would be forever changed and her future fully redeemed.

I am grateful our start doesn't define our finish.

Notes:

Lineage of Royalty - son David

Bathsheba

Bathsheba's story is a bit sordid and understandably messy. But, interestingly some stories with the most checkered beginnings turn out to end fairly well.

The nitty gritty here is that we don't know much about her other than she was a married woman who was involved in an affair with King David. Scripture doesn't tell us how she felt about giving in to the commands of the King because the emphasis of the passages focuses primarily on David. We can speculate why Bathsheba succumbed to the king's advances but in all honesty, we simply do not have the details of her side of the story.

Regardless, she found herself in a mess thanks to David, whose sin trampled on the people around him. Sending Bathsheba's husband to die on the front lines and eventually causing the death of her baby were horrific results laid squarely at the feet of David's disobedience.

This woman in her grief, however, was given a gift from God. She was given a chance to be a part of the birth of Christ. We know David had many wives but Bathsheba was the one God chose to carry the line of Christ forward. We may not know why, but we know He is always right.

Her righteous son, Solomon, built God's holy temple and abounded in great wisdom. He was the legacy of a beautiful woman who experienced intense grief that God allowed. He redeemed her legacy through her son, who would lead to the Son.

David, Bathsheba and Solomon's story teaches us something besides the redemption of sin and wrongs. It teaches us that power and position doesn't make you exempt from sin. They also teach us that despite their status, they still needed a Savior. Just like you and me, they were broken people living in a broken world. Jesus came not just for kings and queens, but for common and poor alike. We cannot escape our need for Christ no matter our social status.

What barriers have you always felt came between you and God? (i.e. worth, status, sin, etc.)

Notes:

David had her husband killed as Bethsheba was pregnant with David the king

Digging Deeper

Use the *Digging Deeper* sections to study further into the Scriptures. These sections are optional but will give you deeper insight and understanding of God's Word.

The Prophecies of Christ

Write out each of the following verses.

Isaiah 7:14-

Therefore the Lord himself shall give you a sign: Behold a virgin shall conceive and shall bear a son, and shall be call Immanuel

Matthew 1:23-

Behold a virgin shall be with child

What prophecy was fulfilled?

not known as being a quiet city

Micah 5:2-

But thou Bethlehem — the ruler shall come forth

Matthew 2:6-

And thou Bethlehem in the land of Judah art not the least among the princes of Juda — for thou shall come come a "Governor" — that shall rule my people

What prophecy was fulfilled?

Scripture Reading:
Luke 1:5-66

Deeper Study:
Luke 1: 67-80

I would venture to say Elizabeth, wife of the godly Zechariah, was a good woman. She is referred to in Scripture as righteous and faithful. If set in our culture we could safely label her a "good church girl." She was from the daughters of Aaron and had priestly lineage within her blood. She was raised to walk in righteousness and taught to follow the law of God without question.

According to His divine plan, Elizabeth became another part of the Christmas story. Her son, John would be a mighty man of God, the forerunner of Christ, and the one to proclaim the way for Jesus (Luke 1:16-17).

I don't know if you are like me but I am a daydreamer. I can riddle up a fantastical story in my head if given a few moments of peace and quiet. When I was pregnant with my children I would think about who they would become, their personalities, and even their accomplishments in life. Imagine for a moment sitting in Elizabeth's shoes mulling over the angelic prophecy given to her husband. Her son would herald the way of the long-awaited Messiah! What an honor! She had more information about who her son would be than we could ever dream.

After reading Luke 1:14-17 what stands out to you most about the prophecy concerning John the Baptist? — *a very unlikely choice*

But, even this woman whose son would pave the way for Christ understood Who he was proclaiming. Coming from the priestly line she no doubt had heard the prayers of her people for a Rescuer. The prophecies handed down through the generations about the birth of Christ were certainly memorized within her mind. The Israelites were waiting for the Messiah.

Her role was significant not just in being the mother of John. She was also a confidante and friend to Mary whose precarious situation, most likely, left her a little more isolated and lonely that she would have liked. Elizabeth who had experienced a miracle of God herself, no doubt could relate with excitement to what was happening with the mother of Jesus.

The events leading to Christ's birth gave Elizabeth a story, a testimony of God's faithfulness and divine plan. This "church girl" still needed Jesus to rescue her. She needed to know her eternity didn't rest on her own shoulders but in the arms of the One her son would proclaim, the One he would baptize in the waters of Galilee. Jesus.

Scripture reminds us that we cannot be good enough on our own. There is comfort in knowing that Christ came to be enough for us.

Notes:

_____

_____

_____

_____

_____

Scripture Reading:
Luke 1:26-56

Deeper Study:
Luke 2:1-20
John 2:1-11

As the darkness of night fell, the stars seemed to shine with an unparalleled brilliance. An infant's first cries pierced through the darkness as they rolled over the hills. A precious new mother holding her highly anticipated child cries tears of relief from the pains of birth that overwhelmed her body. This precious infant with the heartbeat of the Creator was cradled in the straw of a manger.

Sometimes we forget that Jesus was Mary's Savior as well. Her body may have brought Christ into the world, but it didn't remove the fact that she needed to be rescued from the grip of sin. The woman who carried the Redeemer of the world would need the ransom paid for her life, just like ours.

Mary's life was modest and plain and to many, she would not have been deemed worthy of her role in the Christmas story. Yet, God chose her for one of the most important tasks in His plan; to safely give birth to the Savior of the world. No pressure, right?

The swaddled baby in her arms was the glorious prophecy being fulfilled. She watched Him grow, wiped His tears, kissed His cheeks, and as any Israelite mother would do, prayed for her son.

Mary was one of many women whose lives would never be the same because our Deliverer was delivered into the world. Women plagued with sickness, sin, and demons were freed from their bondage, and multitudes became whole, forgiven, and healed by the hand of Jesus. Without the birth of Christ their lives would have remained unchanged. Mine too.

Mary, who carried our Savior, needed a Redeemer.

Her life and specifically her obedience is what glorified God. She exemplifies what a humbled and surrendered life can accomplish.

Seeing Christmas through the eyes of Mary means meeting her in the field when Gabriel came to announce God's plan. It is witnessing the birth of our Savior in a manger because there was no room for Him in the inn. Through her eyes it is being an Israelite knowing that God would one day fulfill His promise and then watching it unfold within her arms.

How would your life have remained unchanged without the birth of Christ?

Notes:

To be the choicest chosen you had to be without sin

Her hunched back and frail hands, wrinkled from so many years folded together in prayer, testified of a woman devoted to prayer. I can almost envision her kneeling on the stone floor day after day calling out to God. Herbert Lockyer says this of her, "It was not in some retired nook of the Temple she prayed, or in a corner where females only supplicated to God. She would join openly in the presence of the congregation and pour out her soul audibly in the temple" (All the Women of the Bible).

God allowed Anna, the prophetess, the privilege of telling others that Jesus was coming. The Messiah they were waiting for was on His way. Her time in the waiting wasn't wasted, but useful as she proclaimed more than just our powerful God, she proclaimed the promise to come.

Scripture tells us that she had been a widow for eighty-four years. In her widowed years she committed her life to God with her days spent within the walls of the temple praying and prophesying of things to come.

Then one day, Anna glanced up from her seat in the temple to see Simeon speaking to a young couple holding a baby. They had come to dedicate the child, and she noticed an astonishing look on Simeon's face, radiating joy and praise. He was beholding the Salvation of God, the Messiah. God surely nudged her soul and she knew that this Baby was the Redeemer she had so faithfully prayed for and anticipated.

In faith Anna approached the young family. Her praise flowed unrestrained and her words commanded the crowd around them as she announced the Savior to the people. So many years she had waited and prayed to see Him with her own eyes and here He was, her Redemption. A faithful life devoted to God in prayer was still in need of that child to rescue her soul. A woman who spoke prophetic words still needed Jesus.

She looked into the eyes of her Savior. Her redemption had come.

What to you describes a devoted life to Christ?

Notes:

_____

_____

_____

_____

_____

_____

_____

_____

_____

_____

The Samaritan Woman

Scripture Reading:
John 4

Deeper Study:
Jeremiah 2:13
John 7:37-38
Rev. 21:6

A quiet well, a broken woman, and a Man capable of removing her shame. The Samaritan woman was probably accustomed to the state of her life, and she was definitely used to avoiding people around her and keeping to herself. After all, you don't have to explain your shame when there is no one around to question your sin.

At the well Jesus wasted no time pointing out what He had to offer her in the middle of her sinfulness. He held the gift of living water in His hands and He offered it to her before He even addressed the nature of her sin. The Samaritan woman found out there are no conditions to receiving the living water, only accepting it.

The woman at the well was ignorant of exactly what Jesus was offering to her. In actuality He was offering her new life, extending a way of escape from the bondage she had chosen for herself. This Living Water was her eternal answer.

No doubt He looked into her eyes and saw every sin that clouded her heart and mind from believing. He told her of her sin and addressed the shame she was so desperately trying to hide.

This Living Water stood ready to wash away all her isolating shame and guilt.

The reason for Jesus's birth as flesh and blood (but fully God) was to address our shame. He came with the sole purpose of redeeming, saving and making whole what was very broken. He came to provide what was needed to bring us into eternity, and to quench a thirst within us that could never be satisfied apart from Himself.

This woman at the well witnessed the truth of the Gospel.

We don't know much about her life after the encounter at the well but we do know that many were saved because of her testimony (John 4:39). Her life was drastically altered from that moment forward. There is no doubt that a life-changing encounter with Jesus will leave you totally different than the way you came.

What was the "well" where Christ met you?

This woman's life was changed because Jesus came to redeem.

Notes:

_____

_____

_____

_____

_____

Digging Deeper

Use the *Digging Deeper* sections to study further into the Scriptures. These sections are optional but will give you deeper insight and understanding of God's Word.

Who Christ is

Understanding the fullness of Christ, we must gain understanding in who He is. Let's look at several statements Christ Himself made in the pages of Scripture. Then make note of how it helps you know Him better.

John 1:1 & 14

_____

_____

_____

John 12:35

_____

_____

_____

John 6:51

_____

_____

_____

John 10:11 & 14

_____

_____

_____

John 11:25

_____

_____

_____

John 15:1

_____

_____

_____

Scripture Reading:
Luke 7:36-50

Deeper Study:
Ephesians 2:8
Romans 3:23
Romans 10:9-10

Standing in a crowded room identified not by your name, but by your greatest mistakes would leave most of us with a shamed face. Nevertheless, Scripture tells us of one nameless woman who dared to cross the room and pour out her adoration at Jesus' feet.

A women completely freed, healed and restored by Jesus will run through you like a line backer in order to kneel at His feet. This woman was no exception. She wasted no time going to Him when she learned where He was. Despite who she was, nothing would deter her from pouring out her oil on His feet and weeping with gratitude over the goodness of her mighty Rescuer. This woman was willing to risk rejection and ridicule to worship Him and offer humble thanksgiving for the forgiveness He gave.

Sin will wrap you in bondage, but Truth will set you free.

How has the Truth set you free?

There are so many things I love about this particular passage of Scripture. First, the woman came up behind Him because her shame was far to great to look the Messiah in the face. When we have stepped too far it is reassuring to know we can come with our shame and our hearts bent to God in humility. Her example demonstrates a heart truly humbled before God.

Secondly, she wept and I am pretty sure it was the ugly kind. She was overcome with emotion and this was her way of expressing adoration to the only One who could completely love her.

I am a sinner too, and so are you. In our culture today we may not necessarily enter a room and be called by our sin, but we still wear the shame. We know the sins that are tucked deep down in our past that haunt us. Maybe they have been long forgiven by God, or maybe we have yet to place them within His hands. Whichever the case please know, dear friend, that there is deliverance. Take them from the corner, dust them off and hand them to Jesus. Meet Him humbly at His feet and ask for freedom.

Notes:

_____

_____

_____

_____

_____

_____

_____

_____

Joanna

Scripture Reading:
Luke 8:1-3

Deeper Study:
Luke 23:50-56
Luke 24:1-12

The picture painted throughout the Gospels doesn't often include the women that served within the ranks of the disciples. Each woman had a distinct background, but their lives were commonly healed. Their motives for following Christ as He ministered were due to the fact that their lives were a witness of His magnificent power.

We long to follow the One who redeems our lives.

Joanna's story is short and her mention isn't one that would normally get a spotlight but nonetheless, it is one that speaks immense volume to the role that women played as disciples of Christ.

She didn't follow Him because He was a popular guy, she followed Him because He had redeemed her soul.

In the Scripture reading where are the two locations it indicates Joanna was? Who was she with? Why is this important?

We cannot look past the fact that God allowed these women to be the first to learn of the resurrection. They witnessed the empty tomb before the male disciples and where the first to spread the news that Jesus was raised from the dead.

We as women hold a special place in the heart of Christ, and God allows us to play a significant role in His great story. We are valuable disciples in His eyes. All of these women, Joanna included, teach us that God has something for each of us. Her time with Christ was marked by giving to His ministry, serving alongside Him, caring for Him upon His death, and rejoicing in His resurrection.

Her job may seem small but it didn't lack in importance. Never underestimate the simple, small offerings you give because they all matter to God. If He has healed you, follow Him. If He has restored you, serve Him. If He has given you new life, pour out before Him all you have to offer.

Notes:

_____

_____

_____

_____

_____

_____

_____

_____

_____

_____

If someone were to describe your redemption and life as a disciple in two sentences what would it say?

There must have been something about Susanna that made her worth mentioning in the pages of Luke.

We know that she was a female follower (disciple) of Christ, and we know that He in some way healed her either from sickness or some sort of affliction (Luke 8:2). We also know that she supported the ministry of Jesus and the twelve.

Other than those facts we know nothing else.

But, the lack of information reveals a telling truth that you and I need.

There is power in the simple life. *You don't have to be well known to be worthy.* You don't need fame or great religious standing to receive freedom from sin.

The greatest lesson we can learn from her is that our name doesn't have to be known for our story to have power. Jesus healed her from physical pain, but also the turmoil of sin. In return she committed her life to following Him.

Your name and mine will never grace the pages of the Bible, but it does not change the fact that God has given our stories great power to draw women to Jesus.

Often we crave our name being known, but we are already known to Christ.

How does this truth give you freedom?

The Truth, Jesus, sets us free. Our freedom is found in redemption and the open arms of the cross. Susanna found it, she treasured it and committed her life to it's purpose. Susanna's commitment outweighed her need of being known. How about you?

Notes:

_____

_____

_____

_____

_____

_____

_____

_____

_____

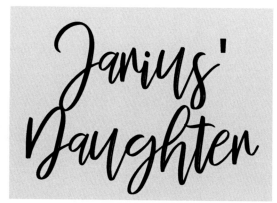

Scripture Reading:
Mark 5:21-43

Deeper Study:
Matthew 9:18-25
Luke 8:41-56

Some times we don't realize our need to be raised to life. We are blinded by the circumstances we have created or ones that are truly beyond our control. We can often see it in others, people who need new life, but how often do we miss it in ourselves.

Jarius, a man who was a leader in the synagogue, was devoted to the law. We can't assume too much about him, but we can venture to guess that he questioned the deity of Christ based on his leadership role. In this moment, however, he recognized Jesus' power and knew that his daughter needed to be raised to life. He knew that the only chance she had was Jesus.

He pressed through the crowd on behalf of her. In desperation as a father, he fell at the Lord's feet and begged for help. When word came to Jarius that the young girl was dead, it did not deter Jesus from stepping in. "As soon as Jesus heard the word that was spoken, he saith unto the ruler of the synagogue, Be not afraid, only believe" (v.36).

Jesus came for her and her parents despite the commotion of those grieving and breathed life back into her body. Scripture says in verse 42 that they were "utterly astounded" by what had taken place. They were amazed by His power. Their daughter that was for a moment dead, was now raised to live again.

When has God's timing been different from your own?

The story of Jarius and his daughter's miraculous resurrection continue to magnify the Father and demonstrate His power and love for us. In our dark and desperate circumstances, God in His timing will bring His perfect resurrection power and breathe new life into our depleted minds and bodies.

He alone can raise us to life.

Notes:

_____

_____

_____

_____

_____

_____

_____

_____

_____

_____

_____

Digging Deeper

Use the *Digging Deeper* sections to study further into the Scriptures. These sections are optional but will give you deeper insight and understanding of God's Word.

More Prophecies of Christ

Write out each of the following verses.

Genesis 49:10-

_____

_____

Luke 3:33-

_____

_____

_____

What prophecy was fulfilled?

_____

_____

2 Samuel 7:12-13-

_____

_____

_____

Matthew 1:1-

_____

_____

_____

What prophecy was fulfilled?

_____

_____

The Bleeding Woman

Just one touch. Simply touching the corner of His robe meant healing and the removal of the sickness that was constantly with her. The dusty road, crowds of people and heat wouldn't stop her because she had heard the whispers that Jesus could do the impossible. He could bind up the wounds she carried every moment of every day and free her from her imprisonment. Determined, she pushed through and reached for Him.

Her silent attempt to touch Him may have been because she questioned her worth, or was it her shame that caused her to remain hidden in the crowd? Nevertheless, she didn't question His power but had faith in His ability to heal.

If we don't believe He came for the broken we will never reach out to touch Him.

How has God proven this truth in your own life? When have you had great faith and not questioned God's power over your circumstance?

The birth of Christ into the world was the beginning of the ultimate cure for our broken state while His death and resurrection are what finally made us whole.

This bleeding woman stood face to face with her Savior, the One who came to heal, but more importantly to redeem. In the end she needed more than just physical healing, she needed Jesus to redeem her life eternally.

When He called her out in the midst of the crowd for touching His cloak she was fearful. Yet, the Son of God's response to her eased her anxiety, "Daughter, your faith has healed you." (v.34)

Despite her fears, our loving God gave her comfort. Reaching out to Christ was an act of faith. He sought to comfort her trembling heart and yet at the same time assure her that never again would she be afflicted by this terrible condition.

Even in our own desperate attempts to run from our present conditions, we forget to simply reach for Christ. Touching His robe or even speaking His name brings peace, hope and, in some cases, healing. At Christmas we long for all of these things. We long to see the Light of the gospel shine above all else. We long for our great hope that is Jesus Christ.

Like the bleeding woman we, too, are desperate for Jesus and the freedom He gives from our brokenness. A brokenness that He came to conquer on a splintered cross.

What does she teach you about your own brokenness?

Notes:

_____

_____

_____

_____

The Adulterous Woman

Scripture Reading:
John 8:1-11

Deeper Study:
Deut. 17-5-6

The air was thick with the desert heat as crowds gathered in front of the temple. Jesus was there teaching when the Pharisees brought her before Him to be judged. This woman caught in the act of adultery was made to stand before Christ, her clothes likely disheveled, her hair uncovered, and her face scarlet with shame.

The Pharisees were more concerned with cornering Jesus than destroying the life of this young woman. She was merely the bait in their trap to gain evidence against Him.

There was no where to hide from her sin and she most likely knew her death was coming. The law of Moses was clear, women like her were to be stoned. By the world's standards she was worthy of death, but in God's eyes she was worthy of life.

Scripture doesn't tell us what Jesus bent down to write on the ground, but for the woman standing before Him it was a line in the sand. It meant her freedom, no one could condemn her but Christ. The Pharisee's who judged her by human standards had no power.

In a world that condemns, Jesus comes to offer forgiveness.

When faced with the reality of our own sin, we can no longer condemn others.

Forgiveness is not a free pass to sin, but freedom from a past of shame.

When the Pharisees walked away from the crowd, Jesus offered forgiveness and instructed her to leave her life of sin behind.

What did God instruct you to leave behind?

The original law was made complete in Jesus, and the punishment that brought peace and freedom to us, rested on Him at the cross. His death paid the price for sin in full thereby fulfilling the law.

This adulterous woman who faced death was redeemed to freedom. Don't let this truth escape you, don't let the deliverance slip through your fingers. The line has been drawn for those who point the finger at your sin. Will your step across the line in the sand toward Jesus, leave the past behind and run to freedom?

No sin is worth bondage.

Make a run for it.

Notes:

_____

_____

_____

_____

_____

_____

_____

Scripture Reading:
Luke 10:38-42

Deeper Study:
John 11:1-45

Mary of Bethany

Our hearts long to be known.

Not just known, but loved.

We long to look the One who loves us the most in the eyes, to worship and adore Him. Mary was the woman who sat on the dusty floor at the feet of the One who came to be her Rescuer. She longed to learn from every word that poured from His mouth because He was God made flesh. She saw no need for the rush of hostessing the way her sister Martha did. Mary only saw the benefit of learning from the Master.

She teaches us something in our season of rush - often our greatest joy and peace come in being still.

What can stillness give you that busyness cannot?

Mary saw the opportunity to savor the redemption in front of her. The stillness gave her time to hear His words and worship at His feet. Not a moment of her time was wasted, despite what her sister had to say and Jesus, Himself, validated her decision, "Mary has made the right choice."

When we choose slow over fast, worship over worry, listening over the rush, and people over projects we will find comfort in the stillness.

This Christmas choose like Mary, less rush and more peace.

In a season built for busy, how can you intentionally slow your pace?

Notes:

_____

_____

_____

_____

_____

_____

_____

_____

_____

_____

Scripture Reading:
Luke 10:38-42

Deeper Study:
John 11:1-45

Rushing, moving, long lists, perfection, order…Martha.

The kitchen was bustling, Jesus was coming! The Messiah would be dining in her home with His friends. The best dinnerware she could find would be stacked on her counters, only the finest food she could find within her means would be served, and the house had to be perfectly tidy. If Martha had a throw pillow she would probably have made sure it was on the seat Jesus would be using with a candle lit next to Him to ensure He could relax while there.

To Martha's dismay, however, her sister Mary's plans looked nothing like candles and throw pillows. She had already picked out her place on the floor at the feet of Jesus. It was too much for Martha's brain to understand and, like normal siblings, someone got tattled on.

Jesus, I am working so hard to serve you while my sister just sits there. Tell her to help me.

Jesus looked at Martha, you are so worried over things that are not important. In this moment there is only one thing necessary and your sister is the only one doing it.

The constant striving left Martha filled with a bitter heart toward her sister, but more than that it left her missing out on the chance to soak up the words of Christ.

What has "busy" robbed you of?

Jesus redeemed Martha from the burden of busy.

He came to redeem us from the trappings of this world - endless striving, demanding perfection and the need to do it all. He beckons our hearts, *come sit at my feet, let me refresh and restore the heart within your chest, and give peace to the thoughts within your mind that have you hurried and burdened.*

Your busyness won't make Him love you more. Sadly, it may keep your pace just fast enough to miss His life-changing truth.

Notes:

_____

_____

_____

_____

_____

_____

_____

_____

_____

Digging Deeper

Use the *Digging Deeper* sections to study further into the Scriptures. These sections are optional but will give you deeper insight and understanding of God's Word.

The Names of Christ

Read the verses and write the name or names of Christ used.

Revelation 1:8 - _____

John 10:11- _____

Hebrews 4:14- _____

Isaiah 7:14- _____

John 1:29- _____

John 8:12- _____

John 1:41- _____

Job 19:25- _____

Luke 2:11- _____

John 1:1- _____

John 15:1- _____

John 8:32- _____

Isaiah 9:6- _____

Scripture Reading:
Luke 8:2
John 20:1-18

Deeper Study:
Mark 16:1-13

Mary Magdalene

It can be difficult to crave freedom when you have never fully experienced captivity. Mary Magdalene was stretched to insanity with her mind tormented by seven demons who held her captive. Likely unable to control her thoughts or emotions, she was trapped in her own body with no way of escape.

The only answer for her desperation was looking directly into the eyes of Jesus. Only Jesus could remove the bondage that held her in chains. Only He could give her new life. While the world saw her as broken, God saw who she *would* be.

She would be a faithful disciple ministering to others who needed hope. This woman who needed freedom so desperately would find herself ministering to Christ at His death and standing at His cross as He gave up His life.

She would also be the first to see His resurrected face. Mary wept at His tomb out of unashamed grief, not for lack of faith, but out of pure love. Love that was born from rescue and deliverance, a freedom that gave her new hope.

What is the new hope Christ has given you?

Mary was given purpose in Christ, and so are you and I. We aren't just redeemed from our mess for nothing, we are redeemed and transformed with purpose. He longs to call us holy and faithful. He changes our story for it to be used for His glory, not kept hidden. Mary didn't have to become a faithful disciple, she could have continued her life in her hometown once she was healed. But, she knew that God had saved her for more. He saved her to *go*.

You and I are also saved to *go*. We are moved beyond our means to share our story and to live everyday as His faithful disciples and walk in new hope.

Notes:

_____

_____

_____

_____

_____

_____

_____

_____

_____

_____

The Poor Widow

Scripture Reading:
Mark 12:41-44

Deeper Study:
Luke 21:1-3

She knew there was nothing to gain in keeping it within her pocket. Giving the offering was far more valuable. Gripping the few coins she has left, she prays and releases them into God's care not knowing what He would do with such a small offering.

As the people came one by one to give, Jesus observed them from close by. Large amounts of money flow into the offering from wealthy hands, but He wasn't impressed. While the rich gave of their extra, she gave of what she truly needed.

The poor widow's faithfulness is found as she drops the coins into the offering box. It takes great faith to give the last of what you have, but it takes even greater faith to believe that despite it being all you have left, God will meet all your needs.

Jesus sees the intentions of our hearts when we give what we have of our treasures. He knows what we have left or what we are holding back that is meant for His glory and purpose. It should be our joy to willingly give what we have because He rescued us from who we were.

Are we giving everything we have within us to the One who redeems us?

Are you willing to give what you have in talents or treasures? What gifts are you bringing as an offering?

Our lives can serve as a testimony and often our actions are what speaks loudest. Jesus took notice of the poor widow because she gave the last of what she had. Her actions spoke of what her heart believed about her Redeemer.

What will your actions say of you?

Notes:

_____

_____

_____

_____

_____

_____

_____

_____

_____

_____

Scripture Reading:
Acts 9:36-43

Deeper Study:
Ephesians 2:10
1 Cor. 12:1-11

The first word used to describe Tabitha in Scripture was *disciple*.

I pray the same will be said of me.

Tabitha was a faithful follower of Christ known for doing good works for others. Yet, in the midst of her faithful work, sickness found her and robbed her of her life.

Even a faithful life requires a Redeemer.

No amount of work we do will remove the sin that is a part of our flesh because we bring no righteousness to the table. Tabitha was a faithful woman whose love for Christ was evident in how she lived and loved others.

Her life in Joppa was redeemed with purpose. The talents placed within her hands by God had value, just as you and I have been given intentional gifts to be used to spread the gospel to the world. "Possibly Dorcus (Tabitha) came to know Christ as her Savior in this church (Joppa), and there caught the vision of how she could serve Christ with her money and her needle." (Herbert Lockyer)

What takes place in verse 39-41 of Acts 9?

According to verse 42 why do you believe these events took place?

Sometimes it isn't just the gifts we have that are a witness but the path God chooses for our lives.

What we must take from here is that the story of our lives being woven by God is for the ultimate purpose of redeeming those around us, those who will see the beauty of God's power pour out of us. The witness of our lives will be evidence of our Creator, our Father, and our Redeemer.

Her talents revealed her love, her healing made her a testimony.

Notes:

_____

_____

_____

_____

_____

_____

_____

Lydia

Scripture Reading:
Acts 16:12-15

Deeper Study:
Romans 1:12
1 Peter 3:15

They were gathered together, each of these women worn from their week's work, in this place of prayer on the Sabbath. As they talked amongst themselves they were joined by Paul and his traveling companions who sought to share the gospel with them. The women sitting there may have heard of Jesus, but it is clear that Lydia's heart was opened to the words Paul spoke. Her life changed in that place of prayer as she heard Paul speak of Christ and the ultimate hope and promise of eternal life.

She became a woman willing to serve and open her home to the disciples, willing to share the hope she found and willing to live a life worthy of the calling as God's child. Lydia, being a dealer of purple cloth, was familiar with royalty, but this King was the only One who would captivate her heart.

What is it about Jesus that captivates your heart?

Scripture says that the "Lord opened her heart to respond" to the words Paul had to say. Not only that, but her family needed it as well, and she shared her hope with them.

Her people.

They came to know Christ and were baptized with her because she was willing to share her story. We can attempt to hide what God has done in us out of fear of rejection, but what goodness we are keeping from our people that we love?

When God changes us the evidence will show and it will be contagious to the people in our lives who are longing for hope.

Be faithful to share the hope you have.

Notes:

_____

_____

_____

_____

_____

_____

_____

_____

_____

_____

Digging Deeper

Use the *Digging Deeper* sections to study further into the Scriptures. These sections are optional but will give you deeper insight and understanding of God's Word.

The women who served with Christ

If we are to study the women of the Bible, we study them not because of who they are, but because of what God did in their lives. Every character of the Bible should be studied in full view of the Gospel. In the section below look at these three specific women and write out why you believe their stories shed led light on the Gospel for us.

Lydia: _____

_____

_____

_____

Tabitha: _____

_____

_____

_____

The Poor Widow: _____

_____

_____

_____

Mary Magdalene: _____

_____

_____

_____

Scripture Reading:
Acts 18:1-22

Deeper Study:
Romans 16:3-5
1 Cor. 16:19

Prisicilla

Priscilla was a woman in the throws of ministry serving diligently and faithfully. She was willing to walk the walk and talk the talk, and she did it alongside her husband, the Apostle Paul and others. In the trenches of serving, these friends worked to bring the gospel to the world. Whatever the cost.

Aquila and his wife, Priscilla, were tentmakers, a common job among Jews. It was of great importance to note they served God in the everyday not just in traveling missions. Together they exemplified what devoted Christian lives look like.

We have seen so many times in a culture that didn't exalt women, how God would use them as incredible ambassadors of the gospel message to the world.

What a privilege we have to continue to be gospel carriers! What does this mean to you?

It cannot be overstated that God's grace has the power to do more in us than we could dream for ourselves. Priscilla and Aquilla went from simple tent makers to mission field workers. We watch God over and over change the stories of our lives as He shapes and molds us into a workmanship of faith and devotion. He continually proves His faithful desire to make us more like Him.

Our lives are made to be a reflection of Him and His redemption. Each mention of our name to the people who love us should remind them of God's grace because He has taken us from brokenness to usefulness.

We are called to walk the life of redemption wherever the mission may take us.

Notes:

_____

_____

_____

_____

_____

_____

_____

_____

_____

_____

Phoebe

A request made to carry a letter. The letter would become one of the foundational books of Scripture - Romans. Phoebe carried these treasured words from her brother in the faith, Paul. This letter she carried with every ounce of care, proved to be one that God ordained to stay intact for generations. Future Christians would draw from its strength and encouragement as they matured in their faith and knowledge of Christ. Her job to deliver this valuable letter to the people who needed it most and carefully preserve it was important to say the least.

God gave women important work within the church serving and working alongside the disciples to carry the gospel into all the world. Phoebe, quite literally, carried the gospel within her hands to people who needed the truth of Christ and direct teaching about their Redeemer.

In Romans 16:2 in the King James uses the word "succorer" to describe her. What words are used in the following translations:

NASB -

HCSB -

ESV -

Pheobe was a helper to many including Paul. She was a benefactor to all believers.

The cause of Christ and furthering the gospel requires all hands, male and female. Each of us given an incredible purpose in the growth of God's Kingdom.

We don't know whether or not Phoebe ever met Jesus in person, but we do clearly know that she was changed and willing to do whatever it took to further the ministry of Christ. No one chooses a life of great cost without being driven by great purpose.

Are you acting as a *benefactor* for other believers?

Are you willing to do the work? What does that work look like to you?

Notes:

_____

_____

_____

_____

_____

_____

_____

_____

_____

Every woman in Scripture teaches us something about ourselves. They teach us that we are worthy, and more importantly how the Gospel changes lives. Each one reveals how Christ impacted their lives whether they knew Him personally or they believed God for His coming. Our story and theirs are woven together in the gospel of Christ. Each one of us is declared holy, beautiful daughters of God because Christ came as a baby, grew into a man, gave His life unto death for our sins, and rose from the grave revealing He is truly who He said He is, our Redeemer.

How has the truth of the gospel changed your life?

What woman in this study has stood out the most to you and why?

Take this truth with you walking forward, Jesus came for you. He came to change your story and rewrite the mess of your heart. God calls *you* His precious daughter. This Christmas as you bask in the busy, the lights, and the sounds of carols playing, be reminded of why He came. Each woman shows us that His life and death were with purpose and freely given for you. Sweet friend, He desires you and all you are, even your greatest mess and He longs to call you holy.

Notes:

_____

_____

_____

_____

_____

_____

_____

_____

Redeemer

Scripture Reading:
Luke 1:26 - 2:20

"For unto us a child is born,
unto us a son is given:
and the government shall be upon his shoulder:
and his name shall be called Wonderful,
Counseller,
The mighty God,
The everlasting Father,
The Prince of Peace."
Isaiah 9:6

Our hearts have wrestled with the weight of our Redeemer. A love like no other, a Rescuer that brings life and freedom from the baggage of sin we carry. A Deliverer, once and for all time, without condition or prerequisite.

Jesus came to earth and walked among us. He came to be within reach of those He intended to save, even the ones who rejected Him. From the moment Mary laid Him in the manger to the moment He took His last breath on the cross...Jesus came to dwell with us.

Our study throughout Advent has shown us example after example of the redemptive power of the One who came to walk this earth. Each story may be different but all have the same outcome - freedom.

The heart of these woman were captivated by Christ alone. Each given a story that would surpass time and speak to our hearts today. There is no escaping the power of their stories, and friend, He has gifted you with a story too. I have no doubt there was a woman in the last few weeks of this study with whom you identified. A woman whose story sounds eerily similar to your own. Just as it was for her, there is also redemption for you.

Write out your story of what redemption means for you and your life.

Notes:

_____

_____

- -

_____

- -

_____

- -

_____

- -

"O Come all ye Faithful"

My dear sweet sister, as we close the book on Advent let us make sure our hearts are open to faithfulness. The faithful women of Scripture each possess a story that God ignites with His power. I pray He has done the same for you.

The same Spirit that dwelled within each of them is within you as well, stirring a fire within your story, urging you to share how God has redeemed your life.

We have been intentional in this season to set our eyes on the One who came to save, rescue and call us redeemed. Not simply redeemed for a moment, but for eternity.

Write 2 Peter 1:3 below.

Each day He walks with us and equips us. He has given us EVERYTHING required for this life. He has supplied what we need to walk in faithfulness, to rest in truth, and to share our stories.

What will you take away from the women we have studied?

Christmas is far more than presents under a tree and twinkling lights, it is an opportunity to point others to our Redeemer.

Write Psalm 107:2 below.

The New Living Translation says it this way, "Has the Lord redeemed you? Then speak out!"

Notes:

_____

_____

_____

_____

_____

_____

_____

_____

_____

Notes

Displaying Grace

Equipping women to thrive in their walk with Jesus.

Follow along with us with the NEW Bible
reading plan. Grab yours FREE at
www.displayinggrace.com

Plus be sure to check out our other resources in
the shop, as well as follow along with us on
social media @displayinggrace

18356776R00038

Made in the USA
Lexington, KY
21 November 2018